FROM
ROLES TO
RESULTS

FROM
ROLES TO
RESULTS

The Human Capital Management Blueprint
for Aligning People, Purpose, & Profit

Tina R. Macon, MA, CBA

Author Name: Tina R. Macon, MA, CBA
Author Email Address:tina@allmacassociates.com
Author's website: https://www.allmacassociates.com/

From Roles to Results, Tina Macon—1st ed.

Dedication

This book is lovingly dedicated to my parents, Frank and Mary Kathryn Allison, who taught me what it means to be a true steward of community, business, and family. Their example shaped my understanding of service, integrity, and purposeful leadership. It is my hope that these pages reflect the spirit of their life's work—the countless ways they partnered with others to uplift lives and improve every space they touched.

The words written by A.B, Androzzo serve as a guiding principle for my life:

"If I can help somebody as I pass along,
  If I can cheer somebody with a word or song,
  If I can show somebody they are traveling wrong,
  Then my living shall not be in vain."
            —Alma Bazel Androzzo (1912–2001),
        American composer, pianist, and songwriter.

Foreword

Leaders in any capacity, and especially Human Resources Management leaders, are confronted daily with complex people management issues. If not resolved promptly and effectively, these issues can result in serious negative outcomes. This book can be a tremendous asset to prevent problems before they arise.

Every new day brings people challenges in the areas of hiring, developing, compensating and retaining key talent. This book addresses each of these challenges and provides straightforward, sound approaches to handle them competently.

Case studies are presented along with proven methods for successfully navigating obstacles that can easily lead managers into trouble for themselves and their organization. The cost of failure can be high - financially, culturally, and in terms of public relations.

Retaining talent is a huge concern today. If your organization is searching for a practical approach for leadership development from within, you'll find feasible options within this book.

Following Human Capital Management principles will ensure that your company's strategies will breathe, live, and thrive.

From Roles to Results -The Human Capital Management Blueprint for Aligning People, Purpose, & Profit is a reference book that should be on every HR leader's bookshelf.

Dr. Linda Gravett

CONTENTS

Acknowledgments

The journey of writing this book has been one of growth, reflection, and profound gratitude. I am fortunate to be surrounded by a wide circle of support, and every person in that circle has played a meaningful role in helping me reach this milestone. There are a few individuals, however, whose contributions I wish to acknowledge with special appreciation.

Dr. Linda Gravett—thank you for being a mentor, coach, and friend. Your steady encouragement and thoughtful guidance have shaped this project in countless ways. As an accomplished author, your insights and feedback have been invaluable to me throughout this process.

Laureece Johnson- your unwavering support and skilled coaching have grounded me during pivotal moments. Your wisdom has strengthened me as a business owner, a leader, and a professional, and I am deeply grateful.

To my children, **Jordan Kenneth and Kathryn Marie Macon**—my greatest hope is that this book inspires you to continue becoming the best versions of yourselves. May it always remind you that you can achieve anything you set your minds to.

To my husband, **Kenneth R. Macon**—thank you for consistently giving me the space to grow, create, and thrive, both professionally and personally. Your love, belief in me, and steady encouragement have been my anchor. I am endlessly grateful for you.

Introduction

Recruiting, managing, redirecting, and terminating—managing people effectively is one of the biggest challenges for any organization. It's not just about filling positions; it's about getting the right people in the right roles and equipping them to succeed. Human Capital Management (HCM) is the strategy that makes that possible—a framework for building and keeping a workforce that fuels long-term growth and consistent results.

Consider a few common situations:

- **The revolving door.** A mid-sized logistics company loses nearly 30% of its staff each year. New hires come in, but poor onboarding, unclear career paths, and disciplinary issues push them right back out. Costs soar, and deadlines slip.
- **The misfit hire.** A nonprofit hires a new program director with great credentials, and a friendly disposition, but no alignment with the actual job requirements. Within six months, the team is frustrated, programs stall, morale takes a hit, and they want to terminate the employment relationship.

- **The promotion pitfall.** A star performer as a team lead in medical billing is promoted to a manager role without training or notification to the rest of the team of the change. Their former peers now report to them, tension rises, and productivity drastically dips as the team struggles with conflict rather than collaboration. The director over the team begins to question their decision to promote and wrestles with whether to demote or fire the employee.

These are everyday realities. Research shows that 83% of businesses struggle to find qualified candidates (SHRM, 2024), while 75% of employees leave jobs due to unclear growth opportunities or poor management (Gallup, 2023). The financial impact is staggering: replacing an employee can cost anywhere from 50% to 200% of their annual salary once you account for lost productivity, recruiting, and training.

And the stakes are rising fast. With the U.S. economy projected to add 6.7 million jobs by 2033, competition for talent will only intensify. Organizations that don't have a strong HCM strategy will find themselves fighting uphill battles—losing critical talent to competitors, overspending on reactive hiring, and watching projects stall because the right skills aren't in place when they're needed. The reality is simple: without a clear workforce strategy tied to your business objectives, hitting growth and revenue goals becomes harder. Customer expectations slip, and profitability suffers.

A lot of leaders find themselves asking, **"How can we attract and keep top talent? Do we know what skills we really need? Can we even afford the people we want to hire?"** This book examines real-world case studies to help you tackle these tricky questions and offers practical ways to figure out what works best for your business. The goal? To help you map out, measure, and master an HCM approach that is customized to your organization and will render the business results needed to Sustain, Grow, and Thrive.

According to the Bureau of Labor Statistics, U.S. total employment is expected to be around 174.6 million by 2033, growing at a rate of 0.4% each year. With this kind of growth ahead, businesses need smart strategies to build a workforce that's both productive and long-lasting. Human Capital Management models help organizations keep their teams strong and steady by carefully analyzing the key tasks and roles each position needs to cover. These models also make sure staffing decisions are tied to the company's revenue goals, creating a shared sense of responsibility for the business's success. Tying these goals into your staffing plans makes it easier to figure out when to hire more people and what that means for your budget.

An effective Human Capital Management (HCM) model design and implementation ensure people are treated as valuable assets. For example, organizations need roles that clearly align with their mission, vision, and strategic business goals, and that alignment must carry through into job descriptions, performance standards, and Key Performance Indicators (KPI's) that define success for both the employee and the organization. When this system is designed strategically and kept aligned with organizational goals and objectives, it does more than fill positions. It helps leaders plan staffing to achieve revenue goals, meet customer expectations, and build a team that's engaged, productive, and ready to innovate.

Failing to invest in building a solid Human Capital Management (HCM) model can lead to lots of issues—high employee turnover, unclear job roles, low morale, and reduced productivity. It can also mean missing revenue goals because you don't have the right skills to attract talent, communicate well, train staff, or bring in new customers. Problems at work, like conflicts between employees who were good friends (both at work and personally) when one is promoted into a leadership role, and the other has to report to them, often pop up when there's no clear HCM strategy in place. These conflicts can be expensive, eating up money through legal fees, wasted time, and extra training. On top of that, poor communication and inconsistent policies can drag down team morale. Instead of focusing on growing the business and keeping customers happy, companies end up stuck trying to fix internal problems.

If your goal is to bring in great employees, keep your team happy, sort out workplace problems, build a strong business foundation, grow future leaders, and make sure everyone's on the same page through solid training, this book is the perfect tool for you. It is packed with straightforward advice on how to set up a Human Capital Management model that helps you identify your organizational needs and tackle employee challenges before they cause bigger issues.

Businesses need smart plans to build teams that work well and stick around to stay competitive. HCM models help connect hiring decisions to business goals, so you'll know when to grow your team and how it fits into your budget. It's not just about HR getting bodies in the seats—it's about making your team a key part of your company's success.

Reading this book will help you solve these problems and build a practical, measurable, and results-oriented plan for your organization. At the end of each chapter, you will have the opportunity to review and apply concepts. The workbook in the Appendix supports strategic application of the concepts outlined in each chapter. I encourage you to use the worksheets with your teams to help build a common focus across the organization.

Using these tools will help you design the HCM blueprint needed for your organization to accurately align your people, processes, and productivity, that will aid in ensuring growth, sustainability, and profitability.

Let's get started!

CHAPTER 1

Infrastructure Building (Problems & Fears)

You've probably lived it more than once: the revolving door. The quiet churn. The onboarding cycle starts with promise and ends with resignation or termination.

You hire with hope. You onboard with optimism. For a moment, it feels like a win—you've found someone sharp, eager, ready to contribute. You imagine them growing with the company, stepping into more responsibility, maybe even becoming a future leader.

And then, barely three months in, it happens.

A meeting. A "can we talk?" An email giving you two weeks' notice. Or, you recognize the person you hired is not the right fit, and it's time to terminate the employment relationship.

Another one's gone. Another role to refill. Another calendar reshuffled. More work is put back on you and the remaining team members. Another investment—of time, of energy, of money—gone before it had a chance to pay off.

When your HCM strategy is out of alignment physically and financially, you're left wondering: Where do I go from here?

Lost Productivity

Every time someone leaves, their knowledge, relationships, and momentum leave with them. The rest of the team slows down—not because they aren't capable, but because they're suddenly navigating gaps in communication, workflow, and execution. Projects stall or get cancelled. Emails go unanswered. Decisions get delayed because the person who was supposed to own them isn't there anymore. What happens to the people who remain? They spend their energy covering instead of creating, and they begin to suffer burnout. It's not just output that suffers—it's innovation, initiative, and the forward movement of the business. All of these areas have a financial impact on the business.

Overtime and Extra Costs

When people leave, money leaks. What started as a single resignation or termination results in a cascade of unexpected costs that could include: job ads, recruiter fees, signing bonuses, onboarding hours, equipment setup, and training time. It also means that covering essential duties can result in increased costs to the business. Meanwhile, you're paying existing staff overtime just to keep things moving—or bringing in contractors at double the cost for half the impact. It's draining your remaining team. And if the next hire doesn't last? You start the whole cycle again.

It's a silent budget drain that rarely shows up on a single line item, but it's bleeding your bottom line all the same.

The Decline of Morale

When people keep leaving, the people who stay start to wonder why. They may not say it out loud, but they feel it. At first, it's disappointment. Then resentment. Eventually, it turns into disengagement. The energy in meetings shifts— less collaboration, more caution. Fewer new ideas, more "quiet quitting." Team members stop investing emotionally because they're not sure who will be around next quarter. Even your top performers begin to pull back, protect their bandwidth, or silently update their résumés. What was once a motivated team starts to feel like a group of survivors—and culture can't thrive in survival mode. Not to mention the financial impact of low morale to the company, which could show up as an increase in sick leave or PTO, longer breaks, and an increase in internal conflicts (e.g., negative tones in conversations —both written and verbal).

Endless Training Costs

Training is an investment—but when turnover is high, it becomes a loss. You pour time, money, and resources into helping new hires succeed. You assign mentors. You create manuals. You host onboarding meetings. And just as they begin to get comfortable—just as they start to adding value— they're gone. All that effort? It doesn't scale. It doesn't compound. It just disappeared. And the team members who trained them? They're exhausted, burned out from onboarding people who never stay long enough to carry their weight. It's not just frustrating—it is unsustainable.

These costs force you, the leader, to shift from vision-casting to damage control—again.

High Turnover

High turnover can quietly erode the performance and reputation of both the employees as well as the organization. To analyze the impact, apply a simple but powerful thinking tool: the **"So What?" Test.**

The **"So What?" Test** is a communication and strategy principle used in consulting, business, and leadership. It pushes every point to its consequence, forcing clarity and urgency. Barbara Minto introduced this approach in The Pyramid Principle (1996) while training consultants at McKinsey. Harvard Business Review has also highlighted the power of asking **"So What?"** to link problems to business impact. By applying it here, you move turnover from an abstract HR metric to a concrete business risk—one that leaders can no longer afford to ignore.

Start with the surface observation—we have to rehire and retrain constantly. Then ask, **"So what?"** The answer: constant rehiring slows projects, increases errors, and frustrates customers. **So what?** Over time, those delays and mistakes drive away top performers, chip away at your ability to retain talent, and weaken your competitive edge.

Reader Considerations: Use the "So-what?" approach when considering the following questions:

How many times in the past year did you onboard someone who didn't last more than six months?

What projects were delayed last quarter because of staffing shortages?

Are your high performers showing signs of burnout?

You don't need me to tell you the emotions these questions spark—you're living them. The frustration of spinning your wheels. The exhaustion of picking up work that should be done by someone else. The fear that competitors are pulling ahead while you're stuck rebuilding—again!

For every employee who leaves, organizations lose an estimated one-and-a-half times their annual salary in lost productivity, overtime, and rehiring costs (Cascio, 2006; Boudreau & Cascio, 2011; Dube, Freeman, & Reich, 2010).

The pain isn't just financial—it's cultural, too.
When employees don't see or understand how they fit into the organization or the impact of their work, they will quickly become disengaged. This means that doing the bare minimum will become the norm. Leaders will be so busy filling in the gaps that there will be no time to consider proper alignment and innovation. Investing the time to

truly identify the skills, talents, knowledge, and experience needed is the key to building a solid foundation for your HCM strategy.

CHAPTER 2

Setting the Foundation

Human Capital Management (HCM) is often viewed as an HR buzzword. When approached correctly, it serves as a strategic foundation that connects people's decisions directly to business outcomes. HCM aligns proper forecasting and budgeting of staff, improves innovation from engaged teams, and supports a clear focus on strategic business initiatives.

What HCM *Is*—and Why It Matters

At its core, Human Capital Management is a strategic, system-wide approach to maximizing the value of your workforce. It's the blueprint for attracting, developing, engaging, and retaining people in ways that align with your organization's mission, revenue goals, and long-term strategy.

HCM is not a single department or a one-time initiative. It is a management philosophy and operating model that ensures people are treated not as expenses, but as assets to be invested in—assets that drive revenue, growth, innovation, and culture. When included in the overall business strategy, HCM integrates every phase of the employee lifecycle—from recruitment and onboarding to leadership development and succession planning—into one cohesive strategy.

> **Example 1:**
>
> A healthcare company facing high turnover in its clinical staff used an HCM model to map out the specific skills and competencies needed for patient care and built sustainable career development pathways that included market-based compensation to attract and retain staff. Within 18 months, retention rose by 32%, and patient satisfaction scores increased by 27%.
>
> **Example 2:**
>
> A manufacturing firm struggling with inconsistent team performance implemented an HCM strategy that ensured role clarity, KPIs, and cross-training. The result? Productivity improved 21% and overtime costs dropped by nearly $400,000 annually.

What HCM *Is Not*—Clearing up the Misconceptions

To truly understand the power of HCM, it's equally important to clarify what it is not: It's not just HR. Human Capital Management is bigger than hiring paperwork, payroll, and benefits. Those are administrative functions.

HCM is a strategic discipline that connects strategic business goals & objectives, revenue targets, and talent decisions to business growth.

It's not a one-size-fits-all model. Every organization's HCM model should be tailored to its unique goals, industry, and workforce dynamics. Taking the time to understand the business needs in real-time will ensure your HCM model stays current and keeps pace with changing market trends and demands.

It's not a "soft" initiative. HCM isn't about perks or culture for culture's sake—it's about driving measurable outcomes: revenue, market share, customer satisfaction, employee engagement, and innovation. It should ensure that every role the organization invests in has a direct impact on the strategy focus of the company as well as the impact to revenue goals.

It's not reactive. Business leaders often react to problems after they occur because evaluating the organization's true needs is not done prior to making staffing decisions. HCM examines and evaluates workforce needs, strategic objectives, and revenue goals and develops a targeted approach to meet them before they become costly challenges.

The Core Pillars of Effective HCM

A strong HCM framework is built on several interdependent pillars. Each one is essential to creating a workforce and culture that is skilled, aligned, and prepared to execute the organization's mission.

Strategic Workforce Planning

HCM starts with examining the organization's needs— both current and future. Workforce planning connects organizational strategy with human capital requirements. It identifies future skill gaps, plans for succession, and ensures the right people are in place at the right time and doing the right things.

Role Design and Alignment

Every role in the organization should exist for a reason— to advance the mission, deliver value to customers, and support revenue goals. HCM ensures job descriptions, competencies, and expectations are clearly defined and aligned with strategy. This clarity reduces overlap, increases accountability, and helps employees understand how their work contributes to larger outcomes. It also serves as an accurate benchmark for establishing market-driven compensation models.

Talent Acquisition and Development

Hiring is not just about filling vacancies—it's about acquiring the right experience, skills, and knowledge to help drive the organization forward. HCM strategies define what "great" looks like for each role and help build talent pipelines accordingly. Beyond recruitment, this pillar includes robust onboarding, continuous learning, leadership development, and career growth programs that keep employees engaged and equipped to excel.

Performance and Accountability Systems

What gets measured gets managed. Effective HCM uses KPIs, performance metrics, and feedback loops to ensure employees meet expectations and contribute to key objectives. These systems provide data to make better decisions about promotions, training, or restructuring—and they create a culture where high performance is recognized and rewarded.

Engagement, Culture, and Retention

Engaged employees are the engine that powers sustainable growth. They don't just show up; they contribute discretionary effort, solve problems proactively, and help organizations achieve their goals faster. Research from Gallup consistently shows that business units with high employee engagement see 14%–18% higher productivity and 21% greater profitability compared to those with low engagement. They also experience significantly stronger workforce stability, with 59% lower turnover in high-turnover organizations and up to 51% lower turnover in low-turnover environments. In addition, highly engaged teams demonstrate 78% less absenteeism, which directly translates into fewer disruptions, stronger team performance, and more consistent service delivery.

What this means for organizations is simple: engagement is not a "soft" metric—it is a business imperative. When people are deeply connected to their work and believe their contributions matter, they are more likely to stay, grow, and innovate within the organization. Engagement initiatives—such as recognition programs, leadership visibility, transparent communication, and well-designed career pathways—reinforce a culture where people feel valued and supported. And when employees feel that level of investment, they respond by investing back into the organization. People don't argue with their own data. If employees feel seen, heard, and valued for their contributions, they will willingly participate and feel ownership for what they have been hired to do.

Leadership and Succession Planning

No business can scale without leadership continuity. HCM establishes criteria to aid in identifying high-potential employees, prepares them for future roles, and ensures that, when leaders exit, successors are ready. This stability reduces disruption, protects institutional knowledge, and supports long-term growth. It also allows organizations to identify lateral growth opportunities to retain employees who may not be interested in advancing vertically into leadership or managerial roles.

How HCM Solves Business Problems

When implemented well, HCM doesn't just improve HR metrics—it helps identify and solve key business problems:

Revenue Growth: By aligning talent with strategy and revenue growth goals, companies see faster project delivery, better innovation, and stronger customer satisfaction—all of which drive profitability.

Cost Control: well-defined workforce planning, professional development, and retention strategies aid in the reduction of turnover, hiring costs, and training expenses.

Agility and Competitiveness: With a comprehensive HCM strategy, organizations can respond more quickly to market changes and new opportunities.

Risk Reduction: Well-defined roles, clear policies, and leadership development help to reduce legal exposure, compliance issues, and internal conflicts.

How HCM Shapes and Strengthens Culture

Culture isn't built through slogans or perks—it's built through intentional design and reinforcement across the organization. A strong HCM framework creates clarity around roles, accountability, communication, and growth—all of which shape how people behave and collaborate. It reduces friction, improves trust, and fosters environments where employees feel valued and empowered.

When people know what's expected of them, understand how their work matters, and feel supported in their growth, they show up differently. They innovate more, stay longer, and contribute at higher levels. Over time, this transforms culture from a potential liability into a powerful strategic advantage.

The Impact of HCM on Company Vision: What are You Doing and Why do You Exist?

Business leaders' first responsibility is "casting the vision" for the organization. Vision is not a statement printed on a wall or buried in a strategic plan. It's more than just having a mission and vision statement. It is a living declaration of why the organization exists and what it strives to achieve. More than words, vision must be embodied and communicated continuously until every team member can answer: What are we here to do? Why does it matter? How does my role contribute?

It is ensuring that the true purpose and deliverables of the organization are clearly defined and continuously communicated across the organization.

Your HCM model is a key step in building the foundation for your organization to function efficiently and stay consistent in the development, execution, and delivery of products and services to your customers.

Without this clarity, organizations drift. With it, they create focus, alignment, and momentum. A well-designed HCM model ensures that vision does not remain abstract but becomes actionable—guiding how the organization positions itself to operate at the highest standards possible, so it can attract the right talent, develop, and engage a workforce able to produce consistent results. When that is accomplished, customer needs will be met, and revenue goals will be attained.

Quick Check—Is Your Vision Alive or Dormant?

- Do employees repeat the vision in their own words?
- Can frontline staff explain how their role supports it?
- Is the vision reinforced in onboarding, meetings, and evaluations?
- Do leaders use it as a filter for decisions?

If most answers are "no," your vision isn't alive yet.

If you don't know why a role exists, you'll never know if it's successful.

Understanding Needs and Determining Roles

Once your vision is clear, the next step is to translate that vision into the work that must be done to reach and grow revenue. Before you post a job description or schedule interviews, pause and define what you really need.

Start with the question: What's the main purpose of this role? Go beyond the job title and describe the true reason it exists. Is the role about simply performing tasks, or about driving a specific result? For example, a "customer service rep" isn't just there to answer phones—they're protecting your customer relationships and ensuring satisfaction that leads to repeat business. When you know the core business need a role fulfills, you can hire and train with focus.

Next, clarify the main tasks and responsibilities. Most job descriptions become catch-all lists, which creates confusion and turnover. Instead, identify the top three to five responsibilities that matter most for success. **Ask yourself: What outcomes must this role deliver? Which tasks directly support revenue or operational efficiency?** Defining this keeps the role manageable and aligned with company goals.

Every position should answer two critical questions:

1. What is the main purpose of this role?
2. Which business need does this role fulfill?

By defining roles in terms of outcomes rather than just tasks, leaders align positions directly to business growth. Tasks and responsibilities flow naturally from this clarity, helping leaders determine what is truly important versus what can be eliminated, automated, or delegated.

Finding the Right Fit for Your Team

Identifying roles is only half the equation. Leaders must also consider where to find the right people to fill them. This includes internal promotions, external hiring, and partnerships with schools, professional associations, or community networks. The right fit is not simply about skill but about alignment with the company's vision, culture, and long-term goals. Let's examine a few examples.

Role	Direct Contribution	Indirect Contribution	Revenue Impact
Sales Manager	New contracts, expanded markets	Build customer loyalty	Increases top-line revenue
HR Manager	Recruitment, retention, compliance, reduced turnover	Stronger culture, better engagement	Protects against costly fines, reduces turnover costs
Operations Coordinator	Efficient scheduling, workflow optimization	Supports staff productivity	Prevents waste, improves profitability

Aligning Jobs to Mission—Reflection Questions

Every role should have a clear line of sight to the organization's larger mission and revenue goals. Employees are more engaged when they understand how their work contributes to the company's success. Make this connection explicit: share it during recruiting conversations, in job descriptions, and during onboarding. Reinforce it in team meetings and tie it to performance conversations.

When you communicate how each role contributes to the bigger picture—whether it's improving customer experience, increasing production efficiency, or supporting growth—you give employees a sense of purpose. That sense of meaning drives retention, commitment, and better results.

Ask yourself:

- How does the role support the company's purpose?
- What would happen if the role didn't exist?
- Which customers, stakeholders, or teammates benefit most from the work of this role?

Benefits of Human Capital Management (HCM)

Implementing a Human Capital Management model at the foundation stage provides multiple benefits:

- **Clarity** – Everyone understands what the organization does, why it exists, and how their work contributes.
- **Consistency** – Defined roles and responsibilities eliminate confusion and overlap.
- **Alignment** – Roles are directly tied to revenue, customer satisfaction, and strategic goals.
- **Scalability** – With a strong HCM foundation, organizations can grow without losing focus or efficiency.
- **Engagement** – Employees feel connected to a larger mission, which increases motivation and retention.

Key Takeaways

Vision Must Live Beyond Words

A vision statement only matters when it is embodied, understood, and practiced daily. Leaders must ensure every team member knows what the organization does, why it exists, and how their role contributes.

Human Capital Management (HCM) Anchors the Foundation

Your HCM model transforms vision into structure—aligning people, performance, and purpose. It ensures consistency, clarity, and accountability across all levels of the organization.

Roles Define How Vision Becomes Action

Each role should have a clear purpose and measurable connection to business outcomes. When roles are designed around results, organizations operate efficiently and avoid redundancy or wasted effort.

People Commit to What They Help Create

Engagement grows when employees understand how their work connects to the mission and revenue goals. When people see the impact of their contribution, they take ownership of the results.

Alignment Drives Efficiency and Growth

When vision, structure, and people systems are aligned, leaders can scale with focus, improve culture, and strengthen financial performance.

Clarity Prevents Conflict

Most organizational challenges stem from misalignment and undefined expectations. Establishing a clear HCM framework turns confusion into consistency and sets the stage for growth.

Purpose + People = Sustainable Success

If people are your organization's greatest asset, then HCM is the operating system that unlocks their value. It's how strategy becomes execution, how teams stay aligned, and how growth becomes scalable.

In the chapters that follow, we'll break down how to design and implement an HCM framework step by step—translating these foundational principles into actionable systems you can build, measure, and optimize for lasting impact.

"A vision without roles is just a dream, and roles without vision are wasted effort.
Human Capital Management brings the two together—purpose and people—to create sustainable success."

— Tina R. Macon, Founder & CEO,
AllMac & Associates

CHAPTER 3

Aligning People with Strategy

Every organization has goals. But goals without alignment quickly become disconnected activities that drain time, resources, and energy. Strategy is not simply crafted in the boardroom; it lives or dies in the daily execution of people doing their jobs. Aligning people with strategy ensures that every role, every decision, and every performance outcome contributes to the bigger picture. This chapter explores how Human Capital Management (HCM) provides the framework for making alignment real through performance expectations, Key Performance Indicators (KPIs), and accountability.

Why Alignment Matters

Organizations often fail not because the strategy was flawed, but because it was never fully communicated to the workforce. When roles drift into activity instead of impact, effort is wasted, and results stall. HCM ensures that roles remain tied directly to organizational priorities, turning abstract strategy into measurable progress.

> **Strategy doesn't fail in the boardroom. It fails at the point of execution.**

Defining Performance Expectations

For people to align with strategy, they need clarity. Performance expectations must be specific, measurable, and observable. Vague goals like "provide excellent customer service" create confusion, while clear standards, such as "resolve 90% of customer issues within 24 hours," create alignment.

Quick Check—Questions to Clarify Performance

- What result must this role achieve?
- How does success look in measurable terms?
- How will customers, co-workers, and leaders know the job is done well?

The Role of KPIs in HCM

Key Performance Indicators (KPIs) are the bridge between strategy and action. They provide the lens through which leaders can measure progress, identify gaps, and celebrate wins. More importantly, they connect employees' daily activities to the company's long-term objectives.

Examples of role-specific KPIs:

- Sales Representative → New contracts closed, renewal rates.
- Nurse Manager → Patient satisfaction scores, compliance audits passed.
- Operations Coordinator → On-time scheduling, cost per client served.

Strategic Goal	Department Focus	Role-Specific KPI Example	Business Impact
Increase market share	Sales & Marketing	Number of new clients onboarded	Drives top-line growth
Improve efficiency	Operations	Percentage of tasks completed on time	Reduces waste, increases profitability
Strengthen compliance	HR & Administration	Number of policy violations avoided	Avoids costly penalties, protects brand
Enhance customer care	Service Delivery	Customer satisfaction rating	Improves loyalty, repeat business

Accountability Systems

KPIs and performance expectations only matter if they are measured and reinforced. **Organizations must move beyond annual reviews and adopt systems of continuous feedback.** Regular check-ins, dashboards, and coaching conversations ensure that employees stay focused and have the support they need to meet expectations.

Managers become more effective when they act as coaches, guiding performance and helping employees connect their work to the company's mission, rather than simply evaluating at year-end.

The Human Side of Performance

Performance alignment is not just about numbers—it is about meaning. Employees need to understand not only what is expected but also why it matters. When they see the connection between their KPIs and the company's mission, motivation and engagement rise.

People commit to what they help create.

A vision without roles is just a dream, and roles without vision are wasted effort. Human Capital Management brings the two together—purpose and people—to create sustainable success. When individuals see their role connected to the larger vision, they not only understand the "why," but also develop a sense of ownership in the outcome.

"People don't argue with their own data. People commit to what they help create."

This principle transforms passive participation into active engagement. When employees are part of defining goals, measuring progress, and interpreting results, the data speaks directly to their contributions. It's no longer about enforcing compliance—it's about building commitment. That commitment drives accountability, fuels innovation, and lays the foundation for sustainable growth.

The Benefits of Aligning People with Strategy

When people are aligned with strategy, organizations gain:

- **Clarity** – Employees know exactly what is expected.
- **Consistency** – Leaders measure performance objectively.
- **Engagement** – Teams connect daily work to a larger mission.
- **Scalability** – Processes and performance can be replicated as the business grows.

Alignment transforms goals into actions, actions into results, and results into sustainable growth.

Alignment is the bridge between vision and results. Without it, organizations chase activity instead of impact. With it, every person becomes a contributor to strategy execution, and Human Capital Management provides the framework to make that alignment measurable, repeatable, and meaningful.

**Alignment turns strategy from a plan
into performance.**

How Aligned Is Your Organization?

Use the questions below to evaluate your current level of alignment. Be honest—your answers will reveal where gaps may exist and where improvements can be made.

1. **Clarity of Expectations**

   - Do employees know exactly what success in their role looks like?
   - Are performance expectations written, communicated, and reinforced regularly?

2. **Connection to Strategy**

   - Can employees explain how their work connects to the organization's goals?
   - Are KPIs linked to measurable business outcomes, not just activity?

3. **Systems of Accountability**

   - Do you have regular check-ins, dashboards, or other tools for monitoring performance?
   - Is accountability ongoing, or does it only happen during annual reviews?

4. **The Human Element**

   - Are employees given context for why their KPIs matter?

- Do leaders provide feedback, recognition, and coaching beyond numbers?

5. **Scalability and Consistency**

- If the organization doubled in size tomorrow, would your performance system still work?
- Are your measures and processes consistent across departments and roles?

If you answered "no" more than "yes," your organization may be chasing activity rather than impact. Strengthening alignment between people and strategy will help you unlock growth, consistency, and long-term success.

Key Takeaways

Strategy Lives Through People, Not Paper
Strategic plans don't fail in the boardroom—they fail in execution. Success depends on how well leaders translate strategy into daily actions, decisions, and measurable results carried out by people at every level.

Alignment Turns Goals Into Results
Goals without alignment become isolated activities. When people, roles, and systems are aligned through HCM, every task contributes to a shared purpose—transforming activity into meaningful impact.

Performance Expectations Create Clarity

People perform best when they understand exactly what success looks like. Clear, measurable, and observable expectations replace guesswork with accountability and confidence.

KPIs Bridge Strategy and Action

Key Performance Indicators connect individual performance to organizational outcomes. They make strategy measurable, allowing leaders to monitor progress, celebrate wins, and identify improvement opportunities in real time.

Accountability Is Continuous, Not Annual

True alignment requires ongoing feedback and support—not just yearly evaluations. Continuous coaching, dashboards, and performance conversations keep strategy alive and adaptable.

Data Drives Ownership and Engagement

"People don't argue with their own data." When employees participate in defining and measuring their KPIs, they take ownership of their results. Involvement turns compliance into commitment.

The Human Side of Performance Matters

Alignment is not only about metrics—it's about meaning. When people see how their work connects to the organization's mission and vision, they bring passion, innovation, and purpose to their performance.

HCM Makes Alignment Measurable and Scalable

Human Capital Management ensures that strategy is not a one-time initiative but an integrated system. It creates consistency across departments, making alignment replicable as organizations grow.

Alignment Is the Bridge Between Vision, Mission and Results

Without alignment, organizations chase activity instead of impact. With it, strategy becomes performance—and every person becomes a vital contributor to success.

Use the workbook to translate these concepts into concrete actions, priorities, and metrics for your team.

CHAPTER 4

Case Study

The Problem

Bossy Man runs ACY, a seven-year-old U.S. company making healthcare uniforms and protective gear for hospitals. He's dealing with a high staff turnover: 25% of the production team has left in the last six months. They need to increase their staff by 20% to go international, but first have to fix this turnover problem. The headquarters is in a rural area, and it's tough to get candidates even though it's just 30 minutes from the nearest suburb. Online reviews say the work environment is stressful, management doesn't care, and pay isn't great. Turnover is hurting product quality and quantity. Supervisors haven't had time off for six (6) months because of call-offs and terminations, which is hitting morale hard. Bossy Man knows there's a problem, but wants his supervisors and management to sort it out quickly.

Right now, their hiring strategies aren't bringing in the kind of workers they need. They've been using popular online job sites, offering referral bonuses to people who stay at least six (6) months, and even bringing in treats to boost morale. But none of it seems to be doing the trick. Management is wondering: Can they actually find and hang onto good employees? Will workers stay or be discouraged and disgruntled? Should they tweak the job postings to make them more appealing? And given how the market is, can they even afford to hire 20% more staff? Should they consider outsourcing, and how would that impact their staffing model and hiring budget?

Have you ever felt stuck dealing with constant employee turnover and not knowing how to fix it? Let me show you how ALLMAC & Associates helped ACY figure out what they needed and created a simple, practical plan to meet their goals for growing, keeping staff, and moving forward.

Understanding the Problem

We helped Bossy Man and his team figure out what they needed by using an impact-to-outcomes method. Here's how we did it for ACY and the main questions every business leader should think about.

What is the Main Purpose of this Role?
Think past the job title and get to the real reason this role exists. Are you hiring a customer service rep just to answer calls, or do you need someone who can keep customers happy and fix issues the right way?

Ask yourself: Do you have a clear idea of what success looks like for this job? Does the employee understand how their work ties into helping your business grow? Without this clarity, you might end up hiring someone who can handle the tasks but doesn't see the bigger picture.

If you're feeling stuck because your employees seem to be "just doing their jobs" instead of pushing things forward, chances are you've missed this important step.

Once you've nailed down the role's main purpose, think about this: "How does this job help the company reach its goals?" Figuring out how the role ties into the bigger picture makes it easier to find the right people and explain what your organization is all about.

What are the Main Tasks and Responsibilities for the Role?

Most job descriptions end up as a long list of random tasks. We wanted to identify the three to five things that really matter for this role.

ACY needed to hire for the role of manufacturing technician. Some key issues we helped them examine included: are they primarily responsible for operating machinery, ensuring quality control, or troubleshooting production issues? If your production team is overwhelmed by handling equipment maintenance on top of their core tasks, perhaps it's time to refine the role to focus on optimizing workflow while delegating maintenance to specialists.

Take a moment to understand the current process and/or flow of work. Are employees being asked to do tasks that don't match their skills? When you focus on the key tasks, it makes it easier to find the right people and keep your team happier since they'll know exactly what's expected of them.

Role: Manufacturing Technician

Step	Action	Purpose
1	Start Shift overview	Begin daily responsibilities
2	Review Maintenance Log	Check for updates, unresolved issues, and scheduled tasks
3	Inspect Assigned Machines	Assess equipment condition and identify potential problems
4	Document Issues Found	Record observations for tracking and follow-up
5	Perform Routine Maintenance or Repairs	Address issues and maintain optimal machine function
6	Test Equipment Functionality	Ensure repairs and maintenance were successful
7	Update Maintenance Records	Keep accurate logs for future reference and compliance
8	End Shift	Conclude daily tasks and prepare for next shift

Visualizing the daily process makes it easier to clarify expectations, spot inefficiencies, and streamline operations for both current employees and new hires.

Does the role need any specific training or education to do it well?

This is a question organizations often skip over. Managers tend to think anyone with experience can do the job, but is that really true in your workplace?

As ACY considered the role of a maintenance technician, we helped them examine key questions: Are you hiring someone just to perform routine checks, or do you need an expert capable of diagnosing complex machinery problems and implementing solutions to prevent downtime? For instance, since they are anticipating international expansion, we had them imagine the factory recently upgrading to automated production systems, integrating innovative robotic arms and predictive maintenance software. A technician with experience in robotics and familiarity with predictive analytics can not only address immediate maintenance needs but also proactively optimize system performance, ensuring smoother operations and reduced costs over time.

To make this role truly effective, the company might organize specialized workshops on troubleshooting utilizing robotic systems or invest in certifications focusing on predictive maintenance tools. This approach not only sets up the new hire for success but also boosts overall productivity, aligning perfectly with the broader company goals.

Finding the Right Fit for Your Team

Think about hiring a machine operator for a manufacturing plant. Are you just looking for someone to push buttons and start machines? Or do you need someone who can troubleshoot issues, ensure quality control, and keep operations running smoothly under pressure? For example, hiring someone with experience operating Computer Numerical Control (CNC) machines can make all the difference in reducing production downtime and improving precision.

What Makes This Role Really Matter?

Take the role of a production supervisor—it's not just about keeping an eye on the assembly line. It could also involve managing schedules, training workers on safety protocols, or finding ways to make workflows more efficient. If your company's goal is to meet high demand without sacrificing quality, this supervisor plays a critical part in ensuring everything runs like clockwork.

Key Areas of Focus:

- Does your quality control team need to know how to use advanced inspection tools, like laser measurement systems?
- What training does your maintenance staff need to handle predictive maintenance software?
- How does the logistics team ensure that shipping aligns with your goals for faster delivery times?

Skills and Training: Are You Asking Too Much?

Let's say your team is switching to automated manufacturing systems. Are you expecting new hires to be experts in these systems from day one? Or your seasoned employees are struggling with software like Enterprise Resource Planning (ERP) platforms because they've never had proper training. Instead of setting people up to fail, identify where your team needs help and provide training or resources to close those gaps. For instance, you could organize a workshop on using robotic arms for assembly tasks or outsource training on specialized maintenance protocols.

Connecting the Job to the Company's Mission

Imagine your mission is to reduce waste in your manufacturing process. Show how each role—from line workers ensuring proper material usage to engineers designing more sustainable production methods—contributes to this goal. When employees see how their work helps the company reach these objectives, they feel more connected. This connection can be emphasized in job descriptions, weekly team meetings, and even during performance reviews.

The bottom line? Whether it's a warehouse worker loading pallets or a production engineer optimizing workflows, every role has to align with your bigger goals. Focus on key tasks, set clear expectations, and give employees the tools they need to succeed. By doing this, you'll build a team that's not just productive but also engaged in making your company a success.

Take a closer look at your manufacturing team. Are employees struggling to learn new systems, like automated sorting machines or advanced inspection tools? Could a focused training session close those gaps? Or is the issue that some hires don't have enough experience with these technologies in the first place?

If people are leaving or seem frustrated, it's worth asking: Are they being expected to handle tasks they weren't prepared for? For instance, is a new hire being asked to manage a robotic welding station without training? Or are experienced hires being thrown into supervising roles that require skills in data analysis they don't have yet? When employees feel unsupported, they're more likely to leave— and that means starting over with hiring yet again.

Outcomes

Once we wrapped up looking at the role, we simplified the job description to make it straightforward and easy to understand. We pinpointed what training was missing to help employees master the key parts of their jobs and made sure everyone understood how this role ties into the company's big-picture goals.

To address this, the company organized workshops for existing staff, teaching them how to use and monitor equipment properly. They also include a training module for new employees, ensuring they are familiar with the technology before stepping onto the production floor. Additionally, Human Resources designed a mentoring program in which experienced employees help train newcomers on advanced inspection tools and software. These mentors were recognized at a companywide meeting and given a monetary gift for their efforts.

This approach not only boosted productivity but also reduced frustration among employees by equipping them with the skills they need to succeed. Over time, the facility saw a significant drop in turnover rates and an increase in employee satisfaction, proving that investing in training pays off.

With everything squared away, ACY was ready to kick off their fresh HCM strategy. They started by focusing on their current team, sitting down with employees to go over the updated job descriptions and offering training where it was needed. They also asked employees for feedback on training, and some of their ideas were folded into the program. To encourage folks to stick around, they offered a referral bonus for bringing in candidates who stayed for at least six (6) months.

Thanks to these changes, ACY hit their goal of boosting staff by 20%, and their turnover rate dropped to just 8%.

Benefits of HCM

Setting up a strong Human Capital Management plan is a smart way for companies to determine exactly what they need to hit their goals. Bossy Man and the ACY team got a solid idea of where they wanted the company to go, the kind of people and skills they needed to get there, and the costs that came with it. In addition, they made the process more rewarding for current employees by letting them help find new hires and earn a little extra cash when those employees stuck around.

Once a company has the right people in place, there is always a chance some issues will pop up. In Chapter 5, we'll dive into how HCM can help handle workplace conflicts.

Key Takeaways

Turnover Is a Symptom, Not the Root Cause
High employee turnover is rarely just about pay or hiring—it reflects deeper issues in clarity, communication, and culture. When people don't understand their purpose, feel unsupported, or see no connection to the mission & vision, they leave.

Clarity Creates Stability
By redefining roles, expectations, and daily workflows, ACY reduced confusion and burnout. Clear job descriptions that identify what matters most empower employees to perform confidently and stay engaged.

Training Turns Frustration Into Confidence
Employees often fail not because they lack ability but because they lack preparation. Structured training, mentoring, and upskilling programs equip teams to meet evolving demands and reduce costly mistakes.

Involvement Drives Commitment

When employees help shape training, job processes, and improvement plans, they take ownership of the outcome. "People don't argue with their own data. People commit to what they help create."

Human Capital Management Connects Roles to Results

ACY's turnaround began when leadership used an HCM framework to connect each role directly to organizational goals—clarifying how individual contributions support productivity, quality, and revenue growth.

Investing in People Yields Measurable ROI

By investing in training and mentorship, ACY cut turnover from 25% to 8% and increased staffing by 20%. Their results prove that Human Capital Management isn't just good for culture—it's good for business.

Recognition Reinforces Retention

Simple acts—like acknowledging mentors and rewarding engagement—build loyalty and motivation. People stay where they feel valued, equipped, and seen.

HCM Transforms Chaos Into Capability

Once ACY aligned roles, clarified expectations, and strengthened communication, they moved from reaction to readiness. With a defined HCM plan, they built the structure to grow the business, sustain processes, improve retention of staff, and scale globally.

The Power of Process Visualization

Mapping out daily steps—like ACY's shift workflow—makes invisible work visible. Visual tools clarify expectations, improve efficiency, and uncover opportunities for improvement.

Success isn't a one-time fix; it's a system. With the right HCM framework, companies can adapt training, hiring, and development strategies to keep people aligned as they scale and evolve.

Use the workbook to translate these concepts into concrete actions, priorities, and metrics for your team.

"People don't argue with their own data. People commit to what they help create."

— Tina R. Macon, Founder & CEO, AllMac & Associates

CHAPTER 5

The Impact of HCM on Workplace Conflicts

"Conflict isn't just personal, it's also structural.
HCM helps turn tension into teamwork."

"Where there are people, there are problems!"

You've probably seen it before—those superstar employees who just can't seem to get along. They're always pointing fingers, complaining about how the other person does their job or runs their department. And when you try to talk it over with them, it's never their fault—it's always the "other person" who's to blame. You might think sitting them down to hash it out would fix everything, but the truth is, that's not always enough.

A solid HCM plan can help sort things out by clearing up miscommunications, making sure everyone knows exactly what their role is, and setting clear expectations so things run smoothly and goals get met. Let's examine what happened at ACY after they hired new team members on the management team.

The Problem

In Chapter 4, Bossy Man and the ACY team identified and agreed on where they wanted the company to go, and who they needed to make it happen: line production supervisors, line staff, an accounting manager, and a quality assurance coordinator. These roles were designed to work together, ensure production demands were met on time and within budget, while keeping quality and safety standards in check.

As part of the company's culture, team leads and managers meet regularly to talk about how things are going, iron out problems, and handle any training gaps. At the end of these meetings, everyone agrees on what needs to be done and who will to take care of it. These meetings happen every Tuesday at 10 a.m. and are supposed to last for one (1) hour.

But there's been a snag. TJ, the line supervisor, keeps showing up late, blaming line issues he has to handle. This means the team has to repeat what's already been discussed, and Liza, the accounting manager, is over it. She's fed up with what she sees as TJ's lack of respect for everyone else's time. On the other hand, Roger, the quality control coordinator, gets where both are coming from but doesn't want the meeting to blow up into another shouting match over priorities, whether it's getting the product out or hashing out Liza's complaints about too much overtime.

Here's the tricky part: TJ reports to the COO, while Liza and Roger report to the CFO. All three of them have gone to their managers, saying the other one is the problem and asking them to find a solution. After a few failed attempts to get everyone on the same page, the company decided to bring in our company to help sort things out and help them figure out a way to work together better as a team.

Our Approach

We helped the senior leaders and their teams figure out why they were clashing by mixing parts of their HCM plan with a simple strengths-and-weaknesses check. Here's how we worked with the ACY team, along with some questions any company should ask to get to the bottom of team issues.

Why is this team so important for helping achieve company revenue goals?

After discussing the collective strength of the group, the team came to an understanding that every member plays a critical role in ensuring production timelines are met, resource use is optimized, and quality standards are upheld. Misalignment can delay output and impact profitability.

> Take a moment to think about your teams. Can you easily see how their day-to-day work ties into the bigger company goals? If not, what might be missing?

How is each person or team contributing to the company's bigger mission?

Utilizing information from the HCM plan, the team was able to clarify how their roles (line supervisors, accounting managers, and quality coordinators) contribute to operational efficiency, cost management, and the delivery of a reliable product to customers.

> Review your HCM strategy to see if everyone's roles and responsibilities are clear and well-defined. Has this been shared with the team in a way they understand?

What happens if we totally miss our goals as a team or business?

Missing production or delivery targets could lead to canceled contracts, monetary losses, and strained relationships with clients and suppliers. It could also lead to job losses across the organization, affecting departmental productivity.

> Have you thought about how disruptions to your business could affect production or customer needs? What would your team need to do to handle those challenges?

What's the fallout if we don't meet the expectations of our customers?

Dissatisfied customers might switch to competitors, damaging market reputation and future opportunities. These are threats to the organization that none of the team members wanted to occur, and they recognized this as an opportunity to come together to ensure the success of the organization and meet the expectations of their customers.

> Take some time to talk with your team about how their work affects the company's results and how customers feel. These conversations can really help everyone see their role in making the company successful.

How much time and money is this problem costing the company?

This is an area that companies don't put a value on. When they do, they begin to understand and quantify the impact of recurring conflicts, such as delays, overtime costs, and reduced employee productivity. We examined each of these topics in detail to help emphasize the urgency of resolving their issues.

> When setbacks occur, it is critical to discuss the impact of the disruption from a financial lens. When employees understand that time is truly money, it will help them reframe their approach to addressing the problem.

What solutions are needed to move forward?

Once they gained consensus on the need for resolution, they began identifying specific areas for improvement, such as better scheduling for line supervisors and setting clear expectations for meeting attendance and ownership on action items.

Take some time as a team to figure out what changes are needed and get everyone on the same page. Once you've agreed on the goal, decide what needs to be done and who will take charge of each task (individually or as a group). After you've wrapped things up, schedule time to debrief on the process and see if anything else needs tweaking. And don't forget to celebrate the wins along the way!

Who is going to take ownership and make changes happen on an ongoing basis?

The team moved to a natural cadence of assignment for accountability. It became apparent who should be in charge of what areas to ensure ongoing monitoring for sustained success.

Guide your team in establishing Standard Operating Procedures (SOPs) to ensure proper accountability, monitoring, and consistency. This will help with onboarding, training, and regular monitoring of how your organization carries out its processes. Set up clear steps and guidelines for accountability, tracking, and staying consistent. This makes onboarding, training, and measuring how things are done much simpler.

How will we evaluate and resolve challenges moving forward?

Moving forward, when challenges began to arise, the team would examine potential risks such as loss of key employees, impact to the customer, lower morale, production inefficiencies, or financial decline. This approach helped them clarify which actions were needed to resolve the issues in the most timely and cost-effective manner. It also helped them identify training needs and use their respective teams to design and implement the training for their teams.

> Regularly checking how things affect the bigger picture will help your team think more strategically. They will start looking at problems from a business perspective instead of just focusing on getting tasks done.

By tackling these questions together, the ACY team stopped worrying about pointing fingers and started focusing on finding solutions. It was all about getting everyone on the same page and moving forward. After resolving some of the big conflicts, the team realized they needed more leaders in the mix so they could share responsibilities better.

Key Takeaways

Conflict Is Not Just Personal—It's Structural
Most workplace tension stems from unclear roles, misaligned expectations, and missing processes—not personality differences. A clear HCM framework addresses root causes and creates systems where people can work together effectively.

Where There Are People, There Are Problems
Conflict is inevitable—but chaos isn't. When organizations expect conflict and plan for it through structured

communication, accountability, and feedback loops, they turn tension into teamwork.

Clarity Turns Friction Into Focus

Miscommunication disappears when employees understand what they are responsible for and how success is measured. Clear job roles, reporting lines, and meeting protocols prevent recurring disputes.

HCM Makes Collaboration Measurable

Using HCM principles, teams can define shared goals, identify overlapping responsibilities, and align performance expectations—reducing frustration and improving coordination between departments.

Every Conflict Has a Cost

Time, morale, and money are lost every time conflicts go unresolved. When teams examine issues through a financial and operational lens, they gain perspective on the true impact of dysfunction and urgency for resolution.

Accountability Requires Agreement

Conflict resolution isn't complete until everyone understands who owns each action step. SOPs (Standard Operating Procedures) and clearly defined accountabilities ensure progress is tracked and sustained.

Communication Builds Connection

Regular check-ins and collaborative problem-solving meetings build trust and prevent blame. When employees are invited to discuss what's working and what's not, solutions become collective rather than corrective.

Leaders Must Model Resolution

Leadership sets the tone for conflict management. When executives approach conflict as an opportunity for growth—not punishment—they create a culture of openness, ownership, and continuous improvement.

People Don't Argue With Their Own Data

When employees participate in identifying problems and defining solutions, they become invested in the outcome. HCM turns disagreement into engagement by empowering people to co-create change.

From Finger-Pointing to Forward Motion

Once the ACY team aligned on purpose, clarified expectations, and established accountability, conflict turned into collaboration. The results were stronger relationships, better communication, and improved performance across the organization.

Use the workbook to translate these concepts into concrete actions, priorities, and metrics for your team.

"Conflict isn't just personal—it's structural. A clear HCM model turns tension into teamwork."

— Tina R. Macon, Founder & CEO,
AllMac & Associates

CHAPTER 6

Developing Leaders from Within: A Practical Approach to Growing Talent

Why Leadership Development Needs a Plan

Great leaders don't just appear when you need them. They aren't born in a staff meeting or discovered in a resume review. Most of the time, they're already in your organization, quietly doing the work—but without the support or structure to step into leadership with confidence.

Without a plan in place to help people grow, businesses fall into the same pattern: promote a top performer, expect them to lead, and hope they figure it out before things fall apart.

Sound familiar?

The Problem

At ACY, this exact situation played out when a longtime line staff member, Chris, who had been employed for five (5) years as a production staffer and team lead, was promoted to a supervisor role. Chris was reliable, fast, and always kept the line moving. He was always willing to help new hires "learn the ropes" and was liked by all of his team members. Naturally, leadership thought he was ready to manage the team. But within a few months, issues started bubbling up: team morale dropped, schedules were falling apart, and turnover ticked back up. Chris wasn't lazy or unmotivated— he just didn't know how to lead. No one had shown him how to coach others, handle conflict, or manage people's energy during a tough production week. He became so frustrated that he was ready to step down from his role and possibly leave ACY. Chris was beginning to feel unsupported, and there was no way to fix the current situation.

> Have you ever promoted someone based on performance and then watched them struggle? Did they have the support they needed—or were they left to figure it out alone?

The solution wasn't to replace Chris—it was to guide him. Once ACY rolled out a leadership track through their Human Capital Management model, things started turning around. They found that Chris needed help with communication, inspiring and managing his team, and tackling higher-level problems. He received hands-on training focused on these areas and started getting regular feedback from both his manager and his team. When tricky situations popped up, Chris learned to break them down and ask for input when needed. He also got coaching from our team to support him as he shaped his leadership style. After just six months, morale improved, turnover dropped, and Chris grew into a strong, confident leader.

> Think about your current team—who has potential to lead but hasn't been given the chance (or the tools)? What would change if they had a clear path to follow?

How Human Capital Management Creates a Roadmap

This kind of transformation doesn't happen by luck. It happens when leadership growth is part of the larger system—when there's a process in place to identify potential, train people before they're promoted, and support them once they're in the role. That's what Human Capital Management (HCM) does.

HCM is about designing the full employee experience, from onboarding to leadership succession. A strong HCM strategy:

- Identifies the key competencies needed at every leadership level
- Provides structured development programs tied to business outcomes

- Tracks progress so growth is visible, measurable, and actionable
- Aligns leadership goals with company strategy

In other words, it removes the guesswork.

> Right now, if someone on your team left or moved up, do you know who's next in line? And more importantly, are they ready?

With the right HCM model, you're not left scrambling. You're building a bench of ready, confident, and capable leaders who already understand your culture, your people, and your goals. That's how you scale. That's how you build sustainably.

Leadership doesn't grow by accident. It grows with intention, structure, and a plan.

> Are you hoping leaders will show up—or are you building them on purpose?

Key Takeaways

Great leaders aren't discovered—they're developed. Without a structured plan, even the most talented employees can struggle when promoted into leadership roles.

Performance and Leadership Are Not the Same

Being great at a job doesn't automatically mean someone is ready to lead others doing it. Leadership requires a different skill set—coaching, communication, problem-solving, and people management.

Structure Prevents Struggle

A Human Capital Management (HCM) framework provides the structure to identify, prepare, and support emerging leaders—before they're promoted. It turns potential into performance through intentional development.

The Cost of Unprepared Leaders Is Costly

Promoting without preparation leads to frustration, turnover, and disengagement. A lack of leadership readiness ripples across the organization, affecting morale and productivity.

Coaching Builds Confidence

Mentorship and Coaching transform new leaders from overwhelmed to empowered. Continuous coaching—before and after promotion—creates confidence and competence that lasts.

HCM Creates a Leadership Roadmap

Through HCM, companies can define competencies, create tiered development paths, and align leadership goals with business outcomes. This makes leadership growth measurable, visible, and sustainable.

Succession Planning Strengthens Stability

When leadership development is integrated into your HCM system, you're never caught off guard. The organization always knows who's next—and that they're ready.

Grow Leaders Who Know Your Culture

Developing talent from within builds loyalty, cultural consistency, and alignment. Internal leaders understand both the people and the mission, making transitions smoother and faster.

Feedback Fuels Growth

Effective leaders are shaped through regular check-ins, progress tracking, and constructive feedback. When development is ongoing, learning becomes part of the culture.

Build Leaders on Purpose, Not by Default

The question isn't, "Who will step up?"—it's, "Who are we preparing to lead?" HCM ensures leadership growth is intentional, strategic, and directly tied to organizational success.

Use the workbook to translate these concepts into concrete actions, priorities, and metrics for your team.

"Leadership doesn't grow by accident. It grows with intention, structure, and a plan."

— Tina R. Macon, Founder & CEO,
AllMac & Associates

CHAPTER 7

How HCM Really Drives Growth and Development Across the Organization

Most leaders think growth comes from sales, marketing, or innovation. And they're right—partly. But here's the reality: none of those things happen without the right people in the right roles, doing the right things, at the right time.

That's where Human Capital Management (HCM) comes in. When done right, HCM is more than hiring and HR policies— it's a strategic growth engine that fuels every department, every initiative, and every dollar earned and spent.

Let's break down how it works.

Growth Starts with the Right People in the Right Places
Hiring isn't about filling seats—it's about placing high-impact talent where they can create the most value. The difference between a company that scales and one that stalls often

comes down to whether leaders treat hiring as a strategic decision or a reactive one.

A strong HCM model looks beyond job descriptions and resumes. It maps out what the organization needs to achieve its goals, identifies the skills and competencies required to get there, and ensures that every role is directly tied to revenue, customer outcomes, or operational efficiency.

> Example:
>
> A healthcare uniform company once came to us struggling with stagnant growth. On paper, they had a strong team and solid sales—but profits weren't increasing. Through an HCM audit, we discovered that nearly 20% of their roles weren't linked to measurable business outcomes. These positions were "nice to have," but they weren't driving revenue or improving efficiency. After redefining responsibilities, reassigning talent, and clarifying expectations, productivity rose 15%—without adding a single new employee.

The lesson? Growth isn't just about having more people. It's about having the right people strategically aligned with your organization's purpose and goals.

Training as a Revenue Multiplier

Many companies treat training as an expense—a box to check during onboarding or compliance season. But forward-thinking organizations see it for what it really is: an investment that multiplies revenue.

When employees are cross-trained, they can fill in during absences, support other departments during busy seasons, and reduce operational bottlenecks. When they're upskilled in high-demand areas, such as data analysis, project management, or customer experience, they create new revenue streams. And when you invest in leadership development, you build an internal bench that's ready to step up, saving time and money on external hiring.

> Example:
>
> A mid-sized logistics company, decided to invest in customer service training for its account managers. The program cost just under $1,000 per employee. Within six months, those same employees were converting customer complaints into upsell opportunities—generating an additional $50,000 in revenue. The ROI? Over 900 %.

Training didn't just improve performance—it directly grew the bottom line.

Culture as a Growth Catalyst

Culture isn't a "soft" factor—it's a revenue driver. A strong, intentional culture reduces turnover, attracts top talent, and fosters innovation. In high-performing organizations, culture becomes a competitive advantage.

HCM shapes culture at every step: from who you hire and how you onboard them, to how you measure success and reward performance. It creates the conditions for people to do their best work—and to want to stay and grow with the company.

> Example:
>
> A tech startup struggling with innovation wanted to understand why their best ideas were always coming from the same small group. A deeper look revealed a culture where speaking up was subtly discouraged—managers often dismissed new ideas in meetings. By redefining performance metrics to reward collaboration and idea generation, the company created psychological safety. Within six months, they saw a 40% increase in employee-submitted product ideas, some of which became their most successful new offerings.

Culture is more than "how it feels" to work somewhere— it's about how people behave and whether those behaviors move the business forward.

Performance Management That Actually Improves Performance

Traditional performance reviews are backward-looking, once-a-year exercises that often do more harm than good. Modern HCM replaces that outdated model with continuous feedback loops, real-time coaching, and data-driven KPIs that focus on growth, not just evaluation.

Continuous performance management allows leaders to spot problems early—before they affect customers, revenue, or morale. It helps identify top performers who are ready for stretch assignments and creates a direct connection between individual contributions and company goals.

> Example:
>
> A client in the manufacturing sector once used annual reviews as their sole performance tool. Issues festered for months, and high performers felt invisible. After implementing a monthly check-in system tied to real-time KPIs, engagement scores rose 27% and output increased 12% in the first quarter.

When employees see the impact of their work—and are recognized for it—motivation soars.

Strategic Workforce Planning

One of the most overlooked elements of growth is workforce planning. Too often, organizations either scramble to hire when demand spikes or overhire, draining cash reserves. Both scenarios are costly.

HCM solves this by aligning workforce planning with strategic goals. Leaders can forecast staffing needs based on revenue projections, run "what-if" scenarios for new products or markets, and design compensation models that scale with growth.

Example:

A healthcare services firm planned to launch two new service lines but had no hiring plan. By modeling different growth scenarios, they realized they would need three specialized roles six months earlier than anticipated.

Proactive planning can prevent delays and enable organizations to hit revenue targets on time.

Breaking Down Silos for Cross-Functional Growth

Departments that operate in isolation slow down growth. Sales doesn't talk to operations, marketing doesn't align with product, and finance only enters the conversation when budgets are due. HCM provides the framework to break those silos by creating shared goals, a common language, and collaborative accountability.

When each team understands how their work connects to broader objectives—and how success is measured across departments—collaboration becomes natural, not forced.

Example):

A mid-sized university was struggling with student retention. Admissions, academic affairs, student life, and career services operated in their own silos—each focused on its own goals and KPIs. Admissions cared about enrollment numbers, academic affairs cared about course completion rates, and career services focused on job placement. There was little communication, and as a result, students were slipping through the cracks.

The university implemented a collaborative HCM framework that aligned all departments around a single, shared goal: increasing student retention by 15%. Roles were redefined, cross-departmental teams were created, and performance metrics were linked to the shared outcome. Within a year, retention improved by 18%, student satisfaction scores rose, and the institution saw stronger alumni engagement, which later translated into increased donations and program funding.

Breaking down silos doesn't just improve communication—it unlocks exponential growth by aligning everyone's work with the same mission.

Measuring the ROI of People Decisions

The final—and often most powerful—component of HCM is measurement. Leaders obsessively measure revenue, profit, and market share, but too few measure the metrics that truly drive those outcomes: the people metrics.

Key measures like revenue per employee, time-to-productivity, employee lifetime value, and turnover cost reveal the financial impact of workforce decisions. Once leaders see these numbers, they stop viewing people as a "cost center" and start treating them as the growth engine they are.

> Example:
>
> An organization discovered that reducing new hire time-to-productivity by just 2 weeks added over $1.2 million to their annual revenue. Another realized that a modest improvement in retention strategy of quarterly employee recognition saved them $750,000 a year in turnover costs.

Understanding the financial impact of workforce planning and employee contributions to the organization helps leaders embrace the mindset that these aren't just nice to have "HR metrics"—they're business metrics that have strategic impact on success and sustainability.

Case Study:

The Situation:
A mid-sized Recruiting & Staffing services company, Do It Right, had ambitious growth goals—to double revenue in three years and expand into new markets. But despite healthy sales pipelines, they kept hitting a wall: missed deadlines, quality issues, and employee burnout. Turnover in their project management and engineering teams was creeping above 20% annually.

The Problem:
Their growth plan was all marketing—no workforce strategy. Job roles were loosely defined, onboarding was inconsistent, and promotions were based more on tenure than capability.

Our HCM Approach:

- **Role Alignment**—redefined job descriptions to link each position to specific business outcomes and revenue goals.
- **Skills Inventory & Gap Analysis**—mapped current employee skills against future service offerings and identified training needs.
- **Leadership Pipeline**—launched a leadership development program for high-potential employees.
- **Performance Metrics**—introduced KPIs tied to client satisfaction, delivery speed, and profitability.
- **Cultural Reset**—refocused hiring and onboarding on collaboration, problem-solving, and ownership.

The Results:

- Turnover dropped from 20% to 9% over 18 months.
- Average project delivery time improved by 25%.
- Employee engagement scores rose by 30%.
- Revenue per employee increased 18%, directly boosting the bottom line.
- Do It Right entered two new markets ahead of schedule.

Lesson Learned:

Growth wasn't stalled by lack of opportunity—it was stalled by lack of alignment between people and business strategy. Once HCM became part of their core leadership conversations, scaling felt less like firefighting and more like following a well-marked roadmap.

HCM-to-Revenue Metrics Every Leader Should Track

- **Revenue per Employee (RPE):** Total Revenue ÷ Number of Employees—shows workforce efficiency in generating revenue.
- **Time-to-Productivity:** Days from hire to full performance—faster ramp-up means quicker contribution to growth.
- **Employee Lifetime Value (ELV):** (Annual Contribution × Tenure) – Hiring/Training Cost—reveals long-term revenue impact per employee.
- **Turnover Cost as % of Revenue:** (Turnover Costs ÷ Revenue) × 100—a high percentage signals money loss and the need for retention investments.
- **Internal Fill Rate:** (Roles Filled Internally ÷ Total Roles Filled) × 100—a high percentage indicates a strong leadership pipeline and cost savings.

> **Quick Leadership Action:** Pick two metrics, benchmark them now, and track changes over the next 6–12 months. Even a small improvement can mean hundreds of thousands—or millions—in retained or generated revenue.

Key Takeaways

- **HCM is a growth strategy, not a support function.** Every decision about people—hiring, training, structure, culture—directly influences revenue, scalability, and competitiveness.
- **Strategic alignment is everything.** When roles, goals, and metrics are aligned with business outcomes, growth accelerates naturally.
- **Investing in people pays exponential returns.** From training and leadership development to cultural alignment and workforce planning, the ROI is measurable and significant.
- **Cross-functional collaboration multiplies results.** Breaking down silos ensures that every department is rowing in the same direction—toward shared outcomes.
- **Measurement turns intuition into strategy.** When leaders track the right metrics, they stop guessing and start making evidence-based decisions that drive profitability and performance.

Use the workbook to translate these concepts into concrete actions, priorities, and metrics for your team.

CHAPTER 8

Succession Planning and Identifying Skill Gaps

Growth isn't just about winning today—it's about making sure you can keep winning tomorrow. For many organizations, the real risk isn't the competition, the economy, or even technology. **It's the lack of a plan for who will step up when key leaders, specialists, or high-performers leave.**

That's where succession planning comes in—and why it must be tied directly to your Human Capital Management (HCM) model. Without it, you're one resignation away from stalled projects, lost customers, and stalled revenue.

HCM gives you the framework to:

- Identify the roles critical to your business strategy.
- Spot the skills needed to perform those roles well—now and in the future.
- Build a talent pipeline so you're never scrambling to replace your most important people.

Succession Planning Is a Growth Strategy

Most leaders think about succession planning only for the C-suite, but in reality, any role that drives revenue, ensures operational continuity, or protects customer relationships is a succession risk. Losing a lead project manager, your top account executive, or a master technician can set you back months—sometimes years.

With HCM, succession planning shifts from a replacement plan to a growth plan:

- You don't just fill a vacancy; you develop people ahead of time to step into higher-value roles.
- You align talent development with strategic goals—so your next leaders are equipped to take the company where it's going, not just where it's been.

Using HCM to Identify Critical Roles

An effective HCM model starts with role mapping:

Define: Identify roles that, if left vacant, would significantly disrupt business performance.

Link to Strategy: Ensure every critical role ties to your revenue model, customer outcomes, or operational stability.

Assess Risk: Evaluate the likelihood of turnover in each role—retirement timelines, promotion readiness, and retention risk.

Example:

A regional logistics company used their HCM framework to map 200 positions. They identified that while warehouse supervisors weren't the highest-paid roles, losing even one could disrupt shipments for major accounts. These became succession priorities.

Identifying Skill Gaps Before They Slow You Down

Skill gap analysis is the backbone of succession planning. HCM makes it systematic:

- Current State: Conduct skill inventories for employees in critical roles.
- Future State: Define the skills those roles will need in 2–5 years based on business strategy.
- Gap Identification: Highlight differences between current capabilities and future requirements.

Common Findings:

- Technical skills may be strong, but leadership and decision-making readiness are weak.
- Employees excel in current systems but aren't prepared for upcoming technology changes.
- Cross-functional knowledge is limited, making transitions harder.

Closing the Gaps

Once you identify the gaps, your HCM model guides how to close them:

Targeted Training: Customizing learning paths for high-potential employees.

Mentoring & Shadowing: Pairing future leaders with current role holders.

Stretch Assignments: Giving emerging talent real projects that expand their capability.

Formal Development Plans: Documenting growth milestones, timelines, and measures of readiness.

Succession planning is strongest when it's ongoing, not a reaction to a departure.

Using HCM, you can:

- Maintain readiness charts that show who's ready now, in one (1) year, or in 3+ years for each critical role.
- Track development progress alongside performance reviews.
- Integrate leadership potential into promotion and bonus decisions.

Case Study:

The Situation:
A mid-sized healthcare network with multiple clinics faced a looming problem: 40% of its senior nursing staff was set to retire within five (5) years. Leadership feared service disruption, increased patient wait times, and loss of institutional knowledge.

The Problem:
There was no pipeline for nurse leaders. Promotions were based on tenure, not readiness, and training was inconsistent across locations.

HCM-Based Approach:

- **Role Mapping**: Identified critical leadership positions across all clinics.
- **Skill Inventory**: Assessed current nurse leaders and high-potential candidates for leadership competencies, regulatory knowledge, and team management skills.
- **Gap Analysis**: Found strong clinical skills but limited budgeting, scheduling, and conflict management experience.
- **Development Plans**: Created a Nurse Leadership Academy with targeted training, mentoring, and stretch assignments.
- **Succession Benchmarks**: Established readiness targets and tied them to annual reviews.

The Results:

- Within two (2) years, 70% of leadership vacancies were filled internally.
- Time-to-fill for leadership roles dropped by 50%.
- Patient satisfaction scores rose as leadership stability improved.
- The program became a selling point for recruiting top nursing talent.

Succession planning isn't just insurance- it's a competitive advantage. By using HCM to tie talent development to strategic goals, this healthcare network turned a retirement crisis into a growth opportunity.

How to Establish Key Performance Indicators (KPI's) Using HCM

- **Start with Business Objectives:** Link every KPI to a strategic goal (e.g., market expansion, higher retention, faster delivery times).
- **Define Role-Specific Outcomes:** Use your HCM role mapping to determine what success looks like for each position.
- **Choose Leading and Lagging Indicators:** Leading predicts performance (e.g., training completion rate). Lagging shows results (e.g., turnover rate).
- **Keep It Measurable and Simple:** Avoid vague goals—use clear metrics like percent of employees meeting role-specific KPI's.

- **Integrate Into Performance Discussions:** Review KPI progress regularly and use them to guide development and promotion decisions.

Examples of HCM-Based KPI's:

- Time-to-fill for critical roles
- Percentage of leadership positions filled internally
- Average employee tenure by role
- Employee engagement index score
- Training ROI (skills gained vs. business impact)

Quick Leadership Action: Pick three KPI's tied to your most critical roles and track them monthly. Use your HCM model to adjust job descriptions, training, and succession plans to hit those numbers.

Key Takeaways

- Succession planning is about growth continuity, not just replacing people.
- HCM provides the structure to align talent readiness with strategic objectives.
- Skill gap analysis ensures your future leaders are equipped for tomorrow's challenges.
- A strong pipeline keeps your business agile, competitive, and resilient.

Use the workbook to translate these concepts into concrete actions, priorities, and metrics for your team.

"If you're not growing your next leaders today, you're gambling with tomorrow's growth".

—Tina R. Macon, Founder & CEO AllMac & Associate

CHAPTER 9

The Story Behind AllMac & Associates

A Legacy of Building Connection, Communities & Contributions

My passion for building AllMac & Associates began long before the company had a name. It began in my childhood, growing up in a family of entrepreneurs who believed deeply in community, connection, and contribution.

My parents, Frank and Kathryn Allison, were serial entrepreneurs in Cincinnati, Ohio. Over the years, they operated businesses in various industries including restaurants, headstone monuments, real estate, and office supplies. But more than the industries they touched, it was their approach that shaped me most. They built businesses that provided employment, partnerships, and opportunities for others. **They believed in solving problems with local resources, uplifting people through work, and giving back through time, sponsorship, and service.**

Community wasn't something they talked about—it was something they lived. My father often reminded me, "You can catch more flies with honey than you can with vinegar." My mother would immediately respond, "Frank, who the heck wants to catch a fly?" Those exchanges still make me smile, but they taught me something powerful: there's always more than one way to see a problem, and every solution begins with perspective.

That early lesson has shaped every part of my professional journey. Across industries—from Corporate, HealthCare, NonProfit, Publishing, and Consulting—the issue of conflict has been a constant thread. Whether the conflict was interpersonal, structural, or organizational, I saw how much time, money, and energy were lost when people and systems were misaligned.

Through my work in Human Resources and Organizational Development, I've studied how effective Human Capital Management (HCM) design can transform that chaos into clarity. When leaders take the time to build systems aligned with their mission, vision, and revenue goals, they create organizations that perform consistently and with purpose. When they don't, they find themselves constantly reacting—casting new visions, changing direction, and losing momentum.

That Understanding Became the Foundation of AllMac & Associates.

We help leaders build sustainable systems that resolve conflict, meet compliance requirements, and align people with purpose. **Our approach is both strategic and human-centered—bridging the gap between organizational goals and the everyday realities of the workplace.** We design comprehensive HCM models that provide measurable frameworks for hiring, training, performance, and development. And because our team is made up of practitioners with deep, real-world experience, we bring practical, tested solutions that work.

Our Services Include:

- **Coaching** leaders and providing effective strategies to develop and lead strong and sustainable teams.
- **Workplace mediation** that assists organizations and staff members through workplace conflict and cultural challenges
- Guiding teams through **company-wide alignment** in decision-making, accountability, and communication.

- **Designing** job structures, performance systems, and recruitment strategies that directly connect to organizational goals.
- Implementing **training and leadership programs** that build capacity and strengthen organizational culture.

Whether in-person, virtual, or hybrid, our work is grounded in one belief: **people are the foundation of every successful organization.**

At **AllMac & Associates**, we don't just consult—we partner. We bring clarity where there is confusion, structure where there is fragmentation, and strategy where there is reaction. Our goal is simple: to **help leaders and organizations turn their vision into action—and their Roles into Results.**

CHAPTER 10

Conclusion- Turning HCM Into Your Competitive Advantage

The truth is, no matter your industry or market, you are facing workforce challenges right now—whether you're talking about them in meetings or not.

- **Retention is harder than recruitment**—great people have options, and they are quicker to leave cultures that don't work for them.
- **Skills are shifting faster than job descriptions**—technology, customer expectations, and market demands evolve daily.
- **Burnout is real**—when employees are stretched thin, morale dips, and engagement drops, all of which hurt productivity.
- **Disconnected cultures slow growth**—when your people don't feel connected to each other or the mission, everything takes longer and costs more.

And here's the thing: you can't "incentive" your way out of these problems with quick fixes like spot bonuses or casual

Fridays. These challenges require a full reset in how you think about, manage, and grow your people—and that's exactly where Human Capital Management (HCM) earns its place as a business-critical function.

The Culture Reset Recipe (HCM Edition)

You can't change culture with slogans, posters, or mission statements alone. Culture changes when you design your people systems to consistently produce the attitudes, behaviors, and performance you want to see—and when leaders model those behaviors daily.

Here's your step-by-step recipe for redefining culture through HCM—complete with real examples.

Clarify the Vision

Get specific: Don't just say "we want a culture of excellence." Define exactly what excellence looks like in everyday actions—how meetings are run, how decisions are made, how customers are treated.

Make it tangible: Turn your cultural values into observable behaviors (e.g., "we respond to client requests within 24 hours," "leaders hold weekly one-on-ones with their teams").

Set non-negotiables: Identify the 3–5 values or behaviors that are essential to your organization's identity and performance, and make them visible in every leadership decision.

Example:

A mid-size consulting firm shifted its culture to "collaboration-first" by making one non-negotiable: every major project had to have cross-functional input before approval. This was added to the project checklist in their HCM system and became part of every manager's performance evaluation.

Align Roles to the Mission

Map roles to outcomes: Use your HCM model to tie every role directly to strategic goals. If a role doesn't clearly contribute to business outcomes, redesign it.

Clarify "the why": Ensure each employee understands how their work drives results.

Audit for alignment: Regularly review job descriptions to ensure they still fit both the business direction and cultural expectations.

> Example:
>
> A regional healthcare provider discovered that several admin roles were spending 40% of their time on outdated reporting processes. After aligning roles to their mission of delivering faster patient care, they invested in an automated reporting system freeing staff to handle direct patient scheduling and improving service times by 25%.

Hire and Promote for Fit and Future
Recruit beyond skills: Hire people who not only meet current technical needs but also embody your cultural values.

Behavioral interviewing: Use questions that uncover past actions aligned with your desired culture.

Promotion readiness: Evaluate candidates on both results and cultural impact.

> Example:
>
> A commercial cleaning company committed to a quality-first culture updated its HCM hiring process to screen for reliability, attention to detail, and a customer-service mindset, in addition to cleaning experience. They used scenario-based questions like, "What would you do if a client pointed out a missed spot just before you were scheduled to leave?"

For promotions, supervisors were selected not only based on efficiency and job knowledge but also on proven leadership, consistent quality scores from client feedback, and their ability to train and motivate teams to maintain high standards.

This approach improved customer satisfaction ratings by 30% in a year and reduced supervisor turnover by half.

Develop the Skills That Drive Culture

Train intentionally: Build programs that strengthen both technical skills and cultural strengths.

Reinforce values in training: Integrate culture examples into onboarding, mentoring, and workshops.

Stretch opportunities: Give high-potential employees projects that challenge them and reinforce values.

> Example:
>
> An energy company striving for a sustainability-first culture designed a Green Leadership Development Program for managers and high-potential employees. Participants attended quarterly sustainability workshops and shadowed environmental compliance officers. They led internal green innovation projects, such as reducing energy waste in office operations or improving field safety protocols for renewable energy sites.

These initiatives were intentionally tracked by Senior Leaders and became part of each leader's performance review, reinforcing sustainability as a daily business priority.

Measure and Reward What Matters

Create culture KPI's: Track metrics such as employee engagement scores, cross-department project success rates, and internal promotion percentages.

Recognize in real time: Celebrate cultural wins publicly.

Align rewards with values: Make sure incentives reinforce the desired culture.

> Example:
>
> A manufacturing company building a "safety-first" culture began publicly recognizing employees who reported potential hazards before incidents occurred. They tracked safety reporting and tied it to quarterly bonuses, resulting in a 40% drop in workplace incidents over one year.

The Transformation Opportunity

When you embed HCM into the core of your business strategy, transformation happens naturally:

- Communication improves because everyone understands their role in the bigger picture.
- Performance rises because expectations are clear and tied to results that matter.
- Morale strengthens because people feel valued, equipped, and part of something meaningful.
- Retention increases because employees see growth opportunities and a culture worth staying for.
- Revenue grows because the right people are in the right roles, performing at their best.

Your Next Move

Don't wait for a crisis—a key resignation, a failed project, or a drop in customer satisfaction—to start rethinking how you manage your most valuable asset: your people.

Instead:

- Audit your current workforce strategy using your HCM model.
- Identify the roles, skills, and cultural gaps holding you back.
- Implement small but intentional changes in hiring, onboarding, training, and performance management that align with your vision.
- Measure the impact—and adjust as you go.

Treat HCM design as an ongoing process—not a project with a finish line. Each pillar strengthens the next, and over time, the system you build will shape a stronger workforce, a more agile organization, and a culture capable of sustaining long-term growth.

Use the workbook to translate these concepts into concrete actions, priorities, and metrics for your team.

NEED MORE HELP?

Contact us at www.allmacassociates.com for a **COMPLIMENTARY** one (1) hour consultation to help you develop your customized Human Capital Management Blueprint to strategically align your PEOPLE PURPOSE AND PROFIT.

Connecting People, Processes & Productivity

About the Author

Tina R. Macon is a seasoned executive with more than 30 years of experience in Human Resources, Labor Relations, Organizational Development, and Business Consulting. As Founder & CEO of AllMac & Associates, she partners with businesses and organizations to strengthen Human Capital Management systems, improve operations, and design strategies for leadership development, executive coaching, conflict resolution, and organizational transformation.

Her client portfolio spans higher education, healthcare, nonprofit organizations, government agencies, small businesses, and Fortune 500 companies. Through this work, Tina has designed and implemented customized programs in leadership development, human capital strategies, conflict management, and change management—helping organizations build stronger teams, enhance performance, and drive sustainable growth.

In addition to her consulting practice, Tina has served as adjunct faculty at the University of Cincinnati, Xavier University, Miami University–Middletown, and Wright State University, teaching courses in negotiation, workplace planning, employee and labor relations, and human resources development. She is also a skilled facilitator, delivering workshops on managerial effectiveness, supervision, conflict management, customer service, time management, team building, and leadership development.

Tina holds a Master of Arts in conflict analysis and engagement from Antioch University McGregor and a Bachelor of Science in labor and human resources management from The Ohio State University. She is certified in EQi, DISC, and Kauffman FastTrac.

An engaged community leader, Tina serves as a Regional Forum Representative for the Women's Business Enterprise Council for the Ohio River Valley region (WBEC ORV). She also serves on the National Board of Directors for the Women's Business Enterprise National Council (WBENC), and the Advisory Board for the Greater Cincinnati Foundation's Women's Fund. She is a founding member of Allies in Action, supporting economic sustainability for Women and Girls in the Greater Cincinnati Region. Tina is a past Commissioner for the Hamilton County Commission for Women and Girls and served on the Board of Trustees for WordPlay Cincy.

Develop Your HCM Blueprint: Workbook & Action Guide

How to Use This Workbook

Your culture is happening whether you design it or not. HCM gives you the tools to design it on purpose—and in a way that grows both your people and your business.

This guided workbook is designed to help you reflect on and apply the key principles of your Human Capital Management (HCM) strategy. Use the prompts, checklists, and planning tables to assess your current practices, identify areas for improvement, and design a clear path forward.

Tips for success:
- Be honest in your responses—this is for your internal planning
- Engage your leadership team or cross-functional partners in discussions
- Revisit your answers every quarter to track progress
- Use the action plan to identify priorities and commit to measurable action steps moving forward

As you begin designing your HCM model, use the following steps to properly align your approach to ensure accurate assessment, alignment, and measurement of outcomes.

Assess Where You Are

Before you design a new system or overhaul existing practices, you need a clear picture of your current state.

Organizational Assessment

Question:	Comments:
How are decisions affecting our staffing model currently made in our organization? Are they strategic or reactive?	
Do we have clear role definitions, job descriptions, and performance expectations?	
Are we anticipating future workforce needs or scrambling to fill gaps?	
What are our current engagement levels, turnover rates, and skill gaps telling us?	

Write down your answers honestly. This baseline will help you and your team measure progress as you implement HCM strategies.

Identify Your Gaps

Rate your organization in the following areas on a simple scale

(e.g., 1 = Needs Major Work, 5 = Highly Effective) in each area:

Category	1	2	3	4	5
Strategic Workforce Planning					
Role Design & Alignment					
Talent Acquisition & Development					
Performance & Accountability Systems					
Engagement, Culture, & Retention					
Leadership & Succession Planning					

The results will reveal areas where the organization is strong and where you need immediate focus.

Connect People Decisions to Business Outcomes

Review your business goals—revenue targets, growth plans, market expansion, and customer satisfaction metrics:

Rate on a scale of 1-5 (e.g., 1 = Needs Major Work, 5 = Highly Effective) in each area:

Business Goal:	1	2	3	4	5
How directly are our people strategies supporting these outcomes?					
Where are misalignments causing delays, missed opportunities, or turnover?					
How can we better link talent planning, development, and retention to those goals?					

The results will reveal areas where the organization is strong and where you need immediate focus.

Start Building the Framework

You don't need to fix everything overnight. Use the insights from your assessments to prioritize your next steps. That might mean rewriting job descriptions to reflect business needs better, launching a leadership pipeline program, or building a workforce plan tied to future revenue projections.

Role Alignment

Which key roles are essential to achieving your growth plan?

Key Roles:	Responsibilities:	Comments

Are the right people in the right seats?
Examine key areas of the organization or by department

Role:	Department(s) Impacted	Comments:
Skill(s) needed:		
Skill gaps:		
Operational misalignments:		

Training & Development

What skills, knowledge, or competencies must be developed to support your organization's strategic goals to meet revenue targets and customer demands?

Organizational Strategic Goal:	Comments
Critical skills gaps:	
Critical knowledge gaps:	
Critical competencies gaps:	
Critical training gaps:	

Training initiatives needed to achieve organizational goals & objectives:

Initiatives to implement:	Objectives:	Target Date	Comments:
Professional development training initiatives to implement:			
Leadership training initiatives to implement:			
Industry training initiatives to implement:			
Skill training initiatives to implement:			

Culture Audit

How well does your current culture support innovation, collaboration, and accountability?

What's working well:	What needs to change:	Comments:

Performance Management

Are performance expectations clear, measurable, and aligned with strategic outcomes?

Current performance metrics: (frequency, delivery style,	Improvements needed:(platform currently utilized, effectiveness)	Comments:

Workforce Planning

How will workforce size, structure, and roles need to evolve over the next 6-12 months?

Projected workforce needs:(tie into strategic goals)	Recruitment or restructuring plans:(tie into revenue goals)	Target Date	Comments:

Cross-Functional Collaboration

Which teams or departments need stronger collaboration to achieve results?

Departments requiring alignment:	Steps to improve collaboration:	Why alignment is needed:	Expected outcomes:	Comments:

KPI Tracking

What Key Performance Indicators (KPIs) will you track to measure success?

Top KPI's to Monitor:	Reporting cadence and ownership:	Importance to strategic business G&O's:	Comments:

Action Plan

Use this chart to outline your top priorities for the organization. Establish ownership, target dates, and follow up needed.

Goal/ Priority	Key Actions	Owner	Target Date	Comments

www.ingramcontent.com/pod-product-compliance
Lightning Source LLC
Chambersburg PA
CBHW060407290526

45791CB00002B/648